SIMPLE MACHINE PROJECTS

Making Machines with Screws

Chris Oxlade

raintree

a Capstone company — publishers for children

Raintree is an imprint of Capstone Global Library Limited, a company incorporated in England and Wales having its registered office at 7 Pilgrim Street, London, EC4V 6LB – Registered company number: 6695582

www.raintree.co.uk
myorders@raintree.co.uk

Edited by James Benefield and Erika Shores
Designed by Steve Mead
Original illustrations © Capstone Global Library 2015
Picture research by Jo Miller
Production by Victoria Fitzgerald
Originated by Capstone Global Library Ltd
Printed and bound in China

ISBN 978 1 406 28929 9
18 17 16 15 14
10 9 8 7 6 5 4 3 2 1

British Library Cataloguing in Publication Data
A full catalogue record for this book is available from the British Library.

Acknowledgements
We would like to thank the following for permission to reproduce photographs: All photos Capstone Studio: Karon Dubke except: Alamy: David Gee 4, 21; BigStockPhoto.com: dragon_fang, 29 (bottom); Dreamstime: Richard Lister, 7; Shutterstock: Boris Bulychev, 4, Diana Taliun, 20, Digoarpi, 9, Isantilli, 29 (top), Julija Sapic, 14, Kondrashov Mikhail Evgenevich, 15, Madlen, 26, RMIKKA, 8, wavebreakmedia, 27.

Design Elements: Shutterstock: Timo Kohlbacher.

We would like to thank Harold Pratt and Richard Taylor for their invaluable help in the preparation of this book.

Every effort has been made to contact copyright holders of material reproduced in this book. Any omissions will be rectified in subsequent printings if notice is given to the publisher.

All the internet addresses (URLs) given in this book were valid at the time of going to press. However, due to the dynamic nature of the internet, some addresses may have changed, or sites may have changed or ceased to exist since publication. While the author and publisher regret any inconvenience this may cause readers, no responsibility for any such changes can be accepted by either the author or the publisher.

CONTENTS

Some words are shown in bold, **like this**. You can find out what they mean by looking in the glossary.

WHAT ARE SCREWS?

You have probably joined together the pieces of a model kit with **nuts** and **bolts**, or fixed a battery cover with a small screw. And you must have put the lid on a bottle. Then screws have helped you.

When scientists use the word "screw", they mean a screw thread, like the thread on a bolt, or on a **fixing screw**. In this book, examples of screws, and practical projects will help you to understand how screws work.

Turning the cap of a plastic bottle makes the top tighten onto the bottle's neck.

Screws around us

Almost every machine and device, from toy cars to giant airliners, has screws that join its parts together. The chairs, beds and tables in your home are also held together by screws.

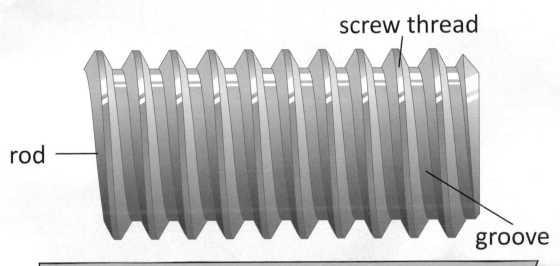

screw thread

rod

groove

 A screw is a rod with a spiral thread around it.

SIMPLE MACHINES

Simple machines help us to do jobs, such as lifting loads and gripping objects tightly. Screws are one of the five types of simple machines. The others are the **lever**, the **pulley**, the **wheel and axle**, and the **ramp** and **wedge**. Also, **springs** are like simple machines.

HOW SCREWS WORK

Remember that when we use the word "screw" we mean a screw thread. Imagine a screw with its thread interlocking with a material. An example of this would be a fixing screw in a piece of wood. When you turn the screw with a screwdriver, the screw pushes or pulls on the material.

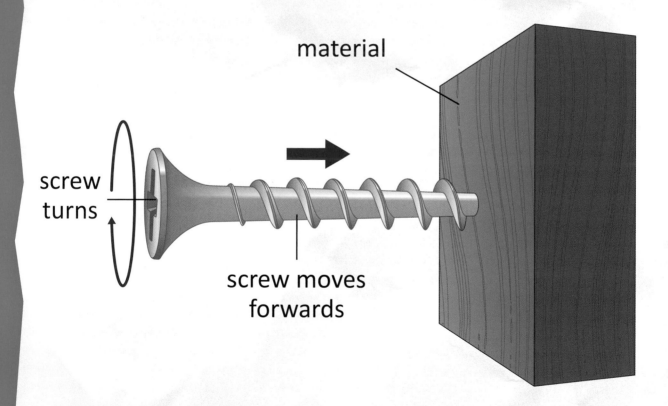

material

screw
turns

screw moves
forwards

 This diagram shows that when you turn a fixing screw **clockwise**, it moves forwards into a material.

When you turn a fixing screw with a screwdriver, the screw forces its way into the wood.

Increasing force

The force a screw makes on a material is greater than the force you use to turn the screw. It is the screw thread that increases the force. That's how a screw can force its way into a hard piece of wood.

FORCE AND MOTION

Simple machines such as screws can change force and motion (movement). A simple machine can make a force (a push or a pull) larger or smaller, or change its direction. It can also make a movement larger or smaller, or change its direction.

FIXING WITH SCREWS

The most common job of a screw is to fix things together. A screw thread can hold an object onto a piece of material, or it can pull two pieces of material against one another.

Screws for gripping

A fixing screw has a sharp end and a wide head. There is a slot in the head that a screwdriver fits into. When you turn a fixing screw, the thread grips the material the screw is in (such as wood or plastic) and pulls itself into the material.

slots for screwdriver

screw thread

This is a fixing screw for wood.

Nuts and bolts

When you turn a nut that is on a bolt, the nut moves along the bolt. Any materials that are squeezed between the nut and the head of the bolt are then held tightly.

Bolt

Nut

Pieces of metal joined together with nuts and bolts.

CLOCKWISE AND ANTI-CLOCKWISE

Most screws have clockwise threads. This means that when you turn the screw clockwise, the screw thread moves the screw away from you. When you turn the screw **anti-clockwise**, the screw thread moves it towards you.

Screw threads

This project will help you to understand how the screw threads on screws work.

What you need:
- some scraps of softwood (such as pine)
- a hammer and small nail
- some small wood screws (about 3 cm long)
- a screwdriver that fits the slots in the screws

WARNING!
Ask an adult for help using sharp objects.

1 Take one scrap of wood. Gently hammer a nail into the centre of the wood to make a small hole.

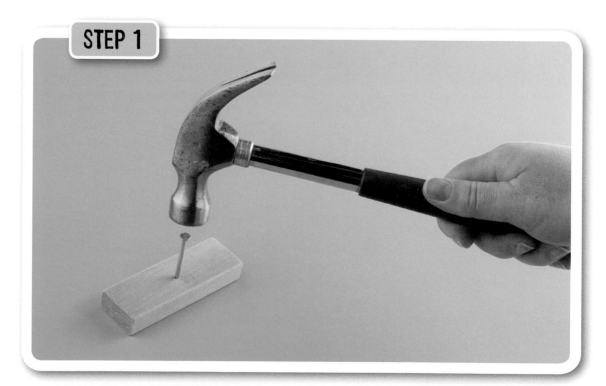

STEP 1

2 Push the sharp end of a screw into the hole you have made in the wood.

3 Insert a screwdriver into the head of the screw and turn slowly clockwise (see picture). You may need to hold the wood and perhaps the screw to begin with.

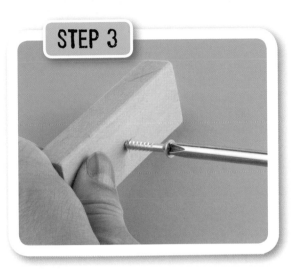
STEP 3

4 Keep turning the screw until about two-thirds of its thread is in the wood.

5 Now turn the screwdriver anti-clockwise to see what happens to the screw.

What did you find out?

When you turn a screw, the thread of the screw pulls the screw into the wood. The thread grips the wood very tightly, so you can't pull the screw out.

Working with nuts and bolts

Try this project to see how the screw thread on a nut and bolt work together.

What you need:
- a bolt (M8 or M10 size) and two matching nuts
- scissors
- some corrugated card
- a sharp pencil

1 Put one nut on the bolt and turn it clockwise until the nut is about halfway along the bolt.

2 Hold the nut and turn the bolt clockwise. Then turn the bolt anti-clockwise to see how the bolt moves through the nut.

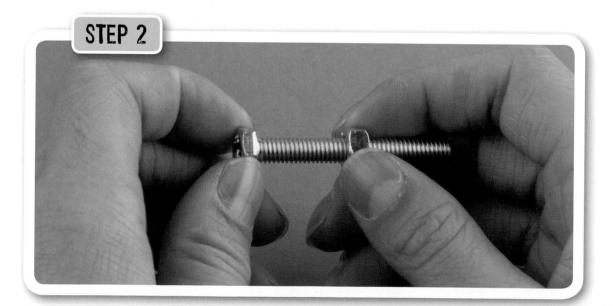

STEP 2

3 Cut two pieces of corrugated card about 10 cm x 10 cm. With a sharp pencil, pierce a hole in the centre of each piece of card.

STEP 4

4 Push the bolt through both pieces of card until the card rests against the nut (see picture). Now put the other nut on the bolt.

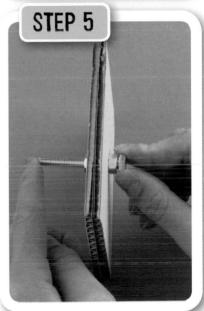

STEP 5

5 Turn the second nut clockwise until it touches the card. Now turn both nuts with your fingers. Find the way of turning the nuts in order to make the pieces of card squeeze together.

What did you find out?

The screw thread on the bolt grips the screw thread on the inside of the nut. Turning both nuts gently with your fingers can squeeze the pieces of card together tightly.

LIFTING AND GRIPPING WITH SCREWS

We sometimes use screws to lift or grip objects. Because screws can make forces larger, you can lift heavy things or grip things tightly by making a small push or pull.

Screw jack

A screw jack is a machine that uses a screw thread to lift a car. This makes changing a car wheel easier. Turning the jack's handle turns a screw thread. This pulls the two sides of the jack together, and this pushes the car upwards.

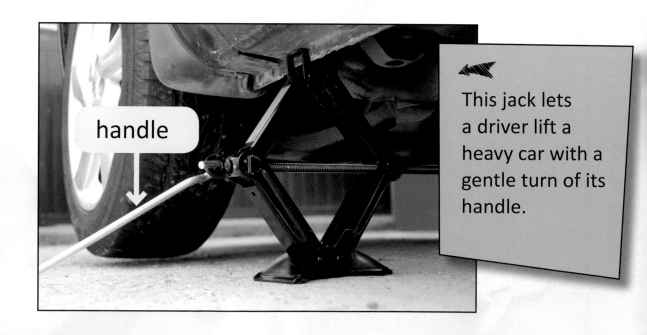

handle

This jack lets a driver lift a heavy car with a gentle turn of its handle.

Vices

A vice is a tool that holds a piece of material while you cut or shape it with tools such as saws and files. You move together the two jaws of the vice by turning a screw thread.

jaws

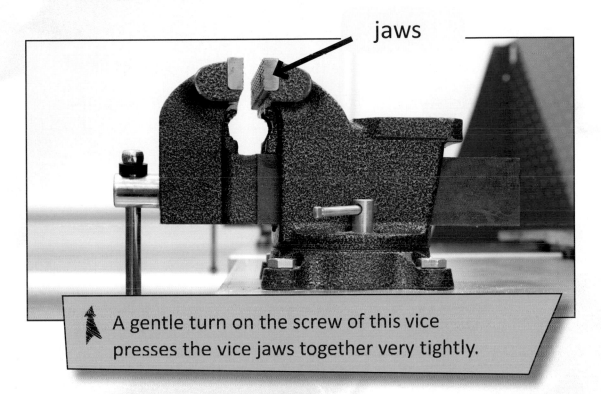

A gentle turn on the screw of this vice presses the vice jaws together very tightly.

PRINTING

For hundreds of years, printing presses had huge wooden screw threads. The screw thread pressed blank sheets of paper firmly onto metal letters covered with ink. This transferred the ink to the paper.

Making a screw jack

In this project, you can make a model screw jack. Use the jack to lift a small plank of wood with just one finger!

1 Cut a square of card about 10 cm x 10 cm. Pierce a hole in the centre of the card with a sharp pencil (see picture). The hole should be slightly smaller than the width of your selected bolt.

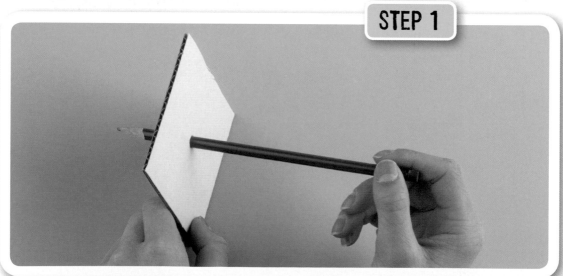

STEP 1

2 Push the bolt through the hole so that the head of the bolt is against the card.

3 Screw a nut onto the bolt until it is tight against the card. You might need to bend the card slightly to make a stable base for the bolt.

4 Put two lolly sticks together face to face. Wrap an elastic band around the sticks about 2 cm from one of the ends (see picture below).

STEP 4

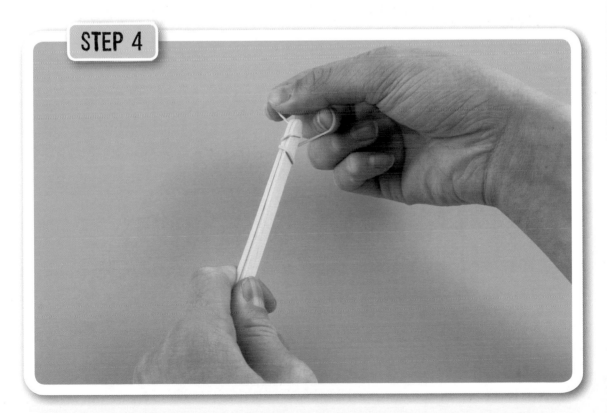

5 Trap the second nut between the two sticks. Push the ends of the sticks together and put an elastic band around these, too. You might need somebody to help you by holding the sticks together.

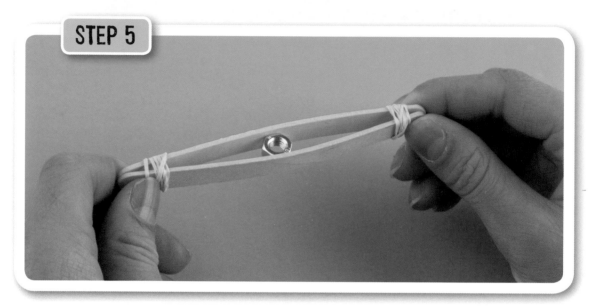

STEP 5

6 Place the trapped nut on the end of the bolt and wind the sticks round and round until the nut is about halfway down the bolt.

7 Put a washer onto the bolt. Then put the pen cap over the washer (see picture, right).

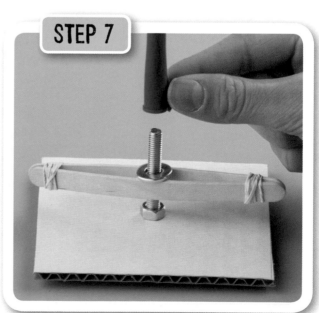

STEP 7

8 Balance the small plank of wood with one end on a heavy book and the other end on the screw jack (as in the picture for step 9).

9 Now carefully wind the lolly-stick handle anti-clockwise to lift the wood (as shown below).

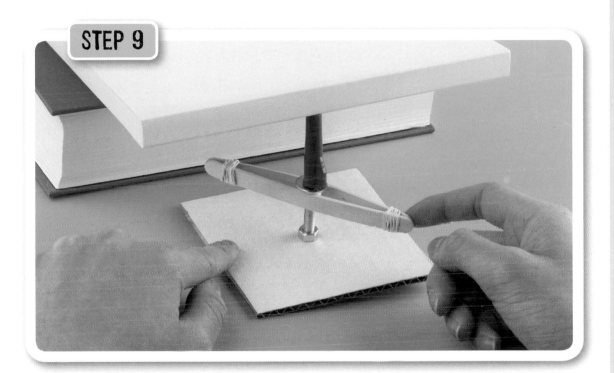

STEP 9

What did you find out?

Try lifting the end of the wood with one finger to see how much force you need. Compare that push to the push you needed on the lolly stick handle to raise the wood. The screw jack made the effect of your small push much larger.

MOVING MATERIALS WITH SCREWS

Screws can also move loose materials, such as powder and beads. A screw thread with a deep groove traps materials between the thread. When the screw turns, the materials are pushed or pulled along the thread.

A soil auger is a screw that moves soil. Construction workers use augers to drill deep holes in soft ground. Drill bits have screw threads that move material out of the hole that is being drilled.

The auger's screw thread lifts the soil from a hole.

SHIP SCREWS

The propellers of ships are sometimes called screws. That's because they work like screw threads, pushing water backwards to move a ship forwards.

Moving liquids

Screws can move liquids, too. A machine called an Archimedean (say "arc-ee-meed-ee-uhn") screw lifts water. It is made up of a screw thread inside a tight-fitting tube. As the screw is turned, the water moves upwards, trapped between the threads.

Archimedean screws are still used in some parts of the world to raise water from rivers onto fields.

Make an Archimedean screw

In this project you can see how a screw thread moves materials when it turns, just like an Archimedean screw.

1 Place the disc (such as a tin) on a piece of card and draw around it. Stand the tube in the centre of this circle and draw around it.

What you need:
- some cardboard
- a disc about 2 cm wider than your tube (such as the base of a tin) to draw round some card
- a cardboard tube (such as the tube from a kitchen roll)
- scissors
- sticky tape
- a large (2 litre) plastic bottle
- some marbles

STEP 1

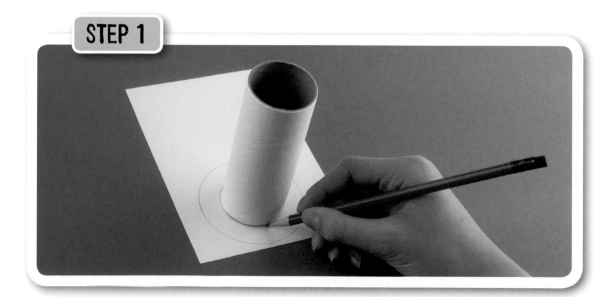

2 Cut out the larger circle. Now cut in from the edge of this disc to the inner circle, and then around the inner circle. You should end up with a ring of card with one cut in it (see picture, right).

STEP 2

3 Put the ring around your tube. Tape one end of the ring to the end of the tube. Tape the other end of the ring to the tube, about 2 cm along the tube from the end.

STEP 4

4 Use a couple of small pieces of sticky tape to attach the ring to the tube. This means the ring stays in the shape of a screw thread.

5 Make another ring in the same way. Fix one end of the ring to the end of the first ring. Fix the other end to the tube, about 2 cm further along the tube.

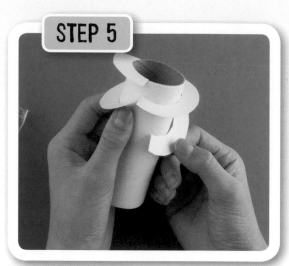

STEP 5

6 Add another two rings in the same way to complete the screw thread (see picture, right).

STEP 6

7 Ask an adult to help you here. Cut the top and bottom off the plastic bottle to leave a tube with parallel straight lines about 15 cm long.

8 Cut a straight line along the plastic tube (see below).

STEP 8

9 Fold the plastic gently around the screw thread. The tube should touch the thread, but not squeeze it. Stick the edges of the tube together.

10 Put the tube on your worktop. Put some marbles in one end of the tube (see picture below).

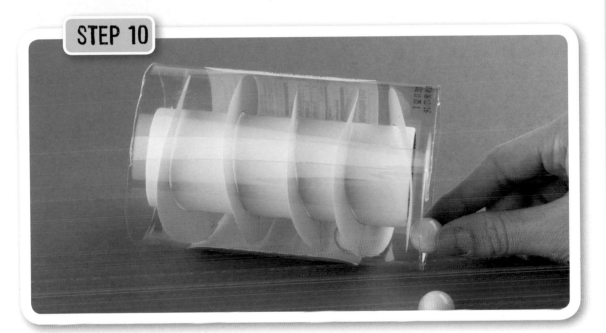

STEP 10

11 Keep the bottle still. Turn the screw clockwise or anti-clockwise. The screw thread collects the marbles and moves them along the tube.

What did you find out?

The screw thread moves the marbles because the marbles become trapped in the thread of the screw. Try turning the screw thread the other way, too.

SCREWS IN COMPLEX MACHINES

Many complicated machines contain screws, too. They can also contain other types of simple machines.

Fixing screws and nuts and bolts hold together the parts of almost all complex machines. These fasteners are often put in place by robots on factory assembly lines. If you have a bicycle, try counting how many nuts, bolts and screws hold it together.

A selection of fixings, including nuts, bolts and fixing screws.

Adjusting with screws

Screw threads are often used to carefully adjust the position of certain parts of machines. For example, binoculars, telescopes and microscopes are all focused using screw threads. When you turn a screw just a small amount, the screw thread moves by an even smaller amount. So the thread can adjust the position of something very accurately.

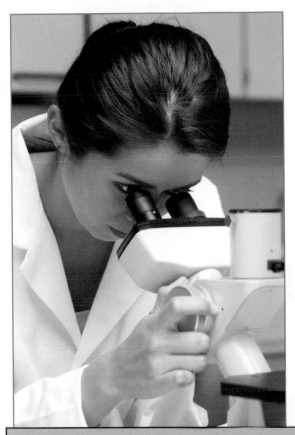

Turning the focusing screw on a microscope moves the lenses very slowly up or down.

LEVELLING WITH SCREWS

Many machines, such as cookers and washing machines, have feet that are fixed on screws. When a foot is turned, it raises or lowers that corner of the machine so that the machine can be made level.

FACTS AND FUN

AMAZING SCREWS

Some of the largest bolts ever made were 8.3 metres (27 feet) long, 1.3 metres (4 feet) in diameter and weighed more than 12 tonnes. They were used to bolt two oil tankers together.

Mountaineers carry special ice screws that they screw into ice. They can tie their ropes to the end of the screw.

Huge augers are used to drill long underground tunnels more than 2 metres (6½ feet) wide for water pipes.

A combine harvester has a screw conveyor at the front. The conveyor gathers up chopped-down crops and feeds them into the machine.

One of the smallest screws ever made is just 1 millimetre long and a tenth of a millimetre across. In your hand, it would look like a speck of dust!

SCREWS TODAY

All simple machines, including screws, were invented thousands of years ago. The screw was invented about 2,000 years ago. At first, screws were used in devices to press olives to make olive oil, and to press grapes for making wine. Screws are even more important today, because they hold together complex machines and so many other things. There's no doubt that screws will be useful for many years to come.

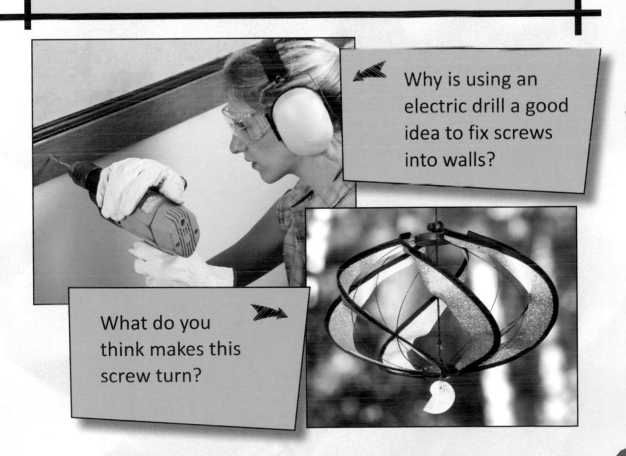

Why is using an electric drill a good idea to fix screws into walls?

What do you think makes this screw turn?

GLOSSARY

anti-clockwise movement in the opposite direction to the hands of a clock

bolt rod with a screw thread and a head at one end

clockwise movement in the same direction as the hands of a clock

fixing screw type of screw used to fix objects to materials, or to fix two pieces of material together

lever long bar that is pushed or pulled against a fulcrum to help move heavy loads or cut material

nut disc of material with a hole in the centre that has a screw thread on the inside, and will fit onto a bolt

pulley simple machine made up of wheels and rope, used to lift or pull objects

ramp simple machine used to lift heavy objects

spring device that can be pressed or pulled but returns to its first shape when released

wedge simple machine used to split apart materials

wheel and axle simple machine made up of a wheel on a rod, used to turn or lift objects

FIND OUT MORE

Books

How Machines Work: The Interactive Guide to Simple Machines and Mechanisms, Nick Arnold (Running Press, 2011)

How Things Work: Simple Mechanisms, Ade Deane-Pratt (Wayland, 2011)

Put Screws to the Test, Sally M. Walker & Roseanne Feldmann (Lerner Classroom, 2011)

Websites

www.edheads.org/activities/simple-machines/index.shtml
Discover more about machines on this website.

www.explainthatstuff.com/toolsmachines.html
This site has some useful diagrams to help explain all about simple machines.

www.galaxy.net/~k12/machines
There are more simple projects to try on this site.

INDEX